aMUSEings

Kristi Worley

BookLeaf Publishing
India | USA | UK

Presentation by *BookLeaf Publishing*

Web: www.bookleafpub.com

E-mail: info@bookleafpub.com

ISBN: 9789358314908

First edition 2023

ACKNOWLEDGEMENT

I would like to acknowledge my friends and family who have encouraged me to write, supported me, and pushed me to challenge myself. I also want to acknowledge you, the reader. I hope you enjoy these poems as much as I enjoyed writing them!

PREFACE

This book is a collection of random poems. They are not connected by a theme or a story, but they are all united by my love of language and my desire to create something beautiful.

Some of these poems are old, and some of them are new. Some of them are long, and some of them are short. Some of them are happy, and some of them are sad. But all of them are a reflection of my inner world, and I hope that you will find something in them that resonates with you.

I Still Feel Lucky

In the corner, by the cement stairs, a spider made
its home on the metal railing.

The brick wall, about waist-high, is crawling
with ants.

Flanking the stairs are roses in bloom. The wind
carries their scent away.

Nearby are the black-eyed Susans, their yellow
petals framing a dark, fuzzy center.

Milkweed stretches toward the sky,

its prickly bulbs being devoured by an army
of aphids.

Dead leaves still cling stubbornly to green
tendrils.

Cicadas scream in the distance.

Ladybugs are good luck, but

A butterfly landed on my shoulder.

I Just Want a Hug

Bitten nails
Buttons in a jar
Pain in my joints
Songs in my head
A collection of keys
Rocks. Lots of rocks
Long pencil shavings
Laundry piled way too high
Recipes, recipes everywhere
Baby teeth (just a few for now)
Not enough spoons to go around
Half empty (or half full?) sketchbooks
Videogames I really need to actually play
Far too many stuffed animals for my own good
Blankets to replace the warmth I don't feel
inside
I could use another blanket
I need more spoons.
I just want a hug

ADHD

In a world that spins with frenzied pace,
Where feelings collide and dreams give chase,
Thoughts scatter like autumn leaves,
Skipping, dancing on a whimsical breeze,
Attention wanders, a nomadic soul,
In search of focus, an elusive goal.

Words become a jumble, a tangled thread,
As concentration wavers, spirit unfed,
Time slips through fingers like grains of sand,
As distractions demand with a beckoning hand.

The mind, a symphony of vibrant hues,
A canvas painted with shades askew,
Impulsivity dances with fiery delight,
Risking, leaping into the unknown night,
Consequences forgotten, adrenaline high,
An endless battle in a tumultuous sky.

Yet amidst the chaos, strength does reside,
A resilience born from the struggles inside,
With compassion and understanding wide,
We stand united, side by side,
For in these struggles, we find our might,
A tapestry woven with colors bright.

Let us embrace the gifts we bring,
In this journey, together we'll sing,
For the struggles of ADHD may define,
But they will never dim our spirit's shine.

ADHD 2

In the realm of ADHD, I'm all over the place.
 One moment I'm writing, the next I'm in space,
I try to stay on task, but oh, what a feat,
My mind is a song that's always off-beat.
I start to clean, but then I see a book,
And suddenly I'm lost, with a curious look.
 ADHD has its fun, like what? I forgot.
Like being a pro at multitasking, (just kidding,
I'm not).
 I can juggle ideas, like a circus performer,
Can I actually learn how to juggle, I wonder?.
Now, where was I? Ah yes, ADHD,
But hold on tight, for we're about to see,
A tangent approaching, from out of the blue,
 Let's dive right in, and see where it takes us to.
Oh, look at that fluffy cloud, shaped like a
sheep,
Reminds me of counting, when I should be
asleep.
Counting sheep leads to dreams, so vivid and
strange,
Like riding a unicorn through a candy cane
range.
 And speaking of candy, who can resist,
The sweet temptation, a sugary twist.

Amidst the distractions, something funny comes
alive,
 A world of possibilities, where laughter can
thrive.
 So let's embrace the chaos, the meandering
mind,
 For in the randomness, treasures we may find.
ADHD, a wild ride that never truly ends,
Hey, look, a butterfly!

Jo

In a haunted house, a girl resides,
Her cat, her only confidant.
For ghosts unseen by human eyes,
Only she and Jo understand.

The girl, with curious heart,
Embraces the eerie ambiance.
Whispers in the night impart,
Stories of a bygone trance.

Jo, her feline companion,
Sees the spirits dance and play.
With emerald gaze, he tracks their motion,
As they guide him through the fray.

In the creaky attic, shadows loom,
A ghostly couple waltzes slow.
In the parlor, a child's laughter booms,
Echoing through the halls below.

One night, a ghost came to her bed,
Its icy hand upon her head.
The girl trembled with fear,
But her cat was always near.

Her cat saw danger in their eyes,
And knew that he must sacrifice,
His tiny body leaped with grace,
To shield her from the ghostly chase.

The ghosts struck with all their might,
But the cat stood firm, a valiant sight,
He fought with courage and with pride,
Until his life force slowly died.

The girl was spared, her savior gone,
But his love for her would linger on,
In the memories that they had made,
And the spirit that would never fade.

Woman of Darkness

I am the woman of darkness,
I am the night's embrace.
I am the shadow's whisper,
I am the moon's disgrace.

I have seen empires rise and fall,
I have witnessed the birth and death of stars.
I have felt the pain of lost love,
And the scars of war.

But through it all, I have remained,
Eternal, as I've watched the elements snuff out
One
By
One.

I am the woman of darkness,
I am the night's embrace.
I am the shadow's whisper,
I am the moon's disgrace.

Crystal Heart

In sorrow's domain, a cursed woman dwells,
A figure formed from crystal's icy core,
No sense of touch, her delicate heart tells,
The ache of longing that she must endure.

Her fragile frame, with beauty to behold,
Reflects the light, a mesmerizing sight,
Yet deep within, a love story untold,
For she can't feel the warmth of love's delight.

No tender kiss, no gentle caress,
Can stir the depths of her passionate soul,
She yearns to feel
Where love's touch can make her spirit whole.

But though denied the sense of touch,
Her spirit soars in realms beyond the veil,
For love's true essence, it can never clutch,
In crystal form, her heart continues to sail.
 For love, you see, transcends this realm,
It flows through veins unseen, in whispers true,
And though this curse may overwhelm,
In spite of it all, her love breaks through.

So let us marvel at the cursed woman's grace,
A testament to love's eternal embrace.

This Child Is...

This child is a tree of protection.
This child is an incomplete embroidery project.
This child is a dreamer of many things.
This child is screams, and tears, and laughter.
This child is bitter and sweet.
This child is silly faces.
This child is a tight squeeze during a meltdown.
This child is lucky number 8... nope, 9.
This child is a scribbled drawing of hearts and flowers.
This child is a collection of stuffed animals of all shapes and sizes.
This child is a pot for cooking instant ramen noodles.
This child is a hug of comfort on a day where I feel broken.
This child is the shadow that follows my footsteps.
This child is a meerkat searching for me when I leave the room.
This child is a mountain of boardgames.
This child is too many hours spent playing Minecraft.
This child is a dance, but only when no one is looking (or so they think).

This child is a cramped bed that can't fit the two
of us.
This child is the ink buried under my skin, over
my heart.
This child is the stretch marks across my
stomach.
This child is the reason I am alive today.

Berry Lane: 2010

Two winters passed as I left Berry Lane
To discover who I am.
I had left loved ones behind.
She was not happy.
I still remember the lashings
From a vindictive tongue.
Though she doesn't recall,
I still bear the scars on my heart.
Should I return home
when she told me to
disappear?
Should I forgive
even though the words
Still slice my heart?
I did, biting my lip until
copper bitterness greeted me.
The door stood open,
Light emerging.
Closer,
Ears ringing,
She was there.
I ran into her open arms,
Cigarette smoke and black coffee woven
into her flannel shirt.

Monster

In human faces, demons wore,
Masks of kindness, hearts impure.
Bruised and broken, she withdrew,
To find peace where monsters grew.

Underneath her bed's embrace,
A creature with a kinder face.
In darkness deep, where secrets tread,
She found love, where fear had fled.

Humans, with judgments, and words like knives,
Scarier than monsters in disguise,
She chose the creature under her bed,
Over the lies that humans spread.

In the quiet of the night,
She let go of the human fright.
In the gloom, love took flight,
Defying reason, embracing night.

Shrouded by darkness, love unfurled,
A balm to heal a wounded world.
For in the arms of the one she chose,
She found a solace no one knows.

Love of Light

A man of light, with a heart so pure,
Was caught in the glow of an elven allure.

His form was a dance of iridescent flame,
In the forest, where the elf girl came.
Her wide eyes, ethereal and bright,
Captured the heart of his radiant light.
His heart, a dance of luminous hues,
Igniting fire that only love imbues.
Born from the rays of the morning sun,
He found in her eyes, a new day begun.

Her elfin grace, enchanting and fair,
With silver strands of starlight in her hair.
He, a being of ethereal glow,
Felt a pull, a love he'd come to know.
His touch, a warmth that dispelled the dark,
Her heart, an ember, ignited a spark.

In twilight's clutch, their worlds aligned,
A symphony of romance they had designed.
He painted her dreams with hues of gold,
In the hymn of love, that would be told.
She, the melody in his luminescent song,
He, the harmony that made her heart strong.

He whispered promises in the morning breeze,
Her laughter echoed through ancient trees.

Love, like light, knows no bounds,
In the realm where magic and wonder are found.

Life and Death

In the realm of elves, where magic flows,
Two sisters dwell, with hearts that oppose.
One held life within her fingertips,
The other wielded death's eclipse.

The elder sister, with envy in her gaze,
Obsessed with the younger's mysterious ways.
In death's grasp, a beauty she found,
A power that echoed without a sound.
The elder sister, with petals of life,
Longed for the shadows, the dance, the strife.
In envy's grip, her heart entwined,
Obsessed with powers of a different kind.
Consumed by coveting,
She sought the death her sister could bring.

Two sisters, bound by fate's design,
One obsessed with the powers malign.
The other, burdened by the shadows she wore,
Cursing her powers forevermore.
The elder's desire, the younger's lament,
Hearts eternally discontent.

A Knell

A siren, with no sweet melody,
Her voice, a tempest in the endless sea.
A symphony of chaos, a dissonant tune,
Beneath the waves, she sought love's boon.

Oh, the siren sang with all her heart,
A cacophony in the tranquil dark.
Her scales shimmered, a forlorn display,
As she crooned, driving sailors away.

Her heart, a ship lost in the night,
Battered by the ocean's might.
The dramatic siren, still she craves,
A soul that calms her stormy waves.

In the deep, where currents swirl,
A tone-deaf siren, a determined girl.
Seeking someone to share her fate,
In the turbulent sea of love, she'll wait.

Crimson

In the realm where flames dance in glee,
Was a fire elemental, wild and free.
A womanizer, with a heart ablaze,
Igniting passions in a fiery haze.

He weaved his charm in cinders' glow,
A heart of flame, a roving soul.
A cascade of embers, a trail of desire,
He played with hearts, a dangerous fire.
With eyes that burned like molten gold,
He left a tale of love untold.

In the nights, his desires roared,
Yet, in the blaze, a void he ignored.
A yearning for a love that lasts,
And soothes the pain and heals the past.

Then, amidst the flickering heat,
A love ignited, oh, so sweet.
A tempest of emotions, a burning storm,
His womanizing heart began to transform.

Her eyes, a reflection of flames sincere,
Igniting a passion, dispelling the fear.
Her kindness, a balm to his restless soul,

He felt a warmth that made him whole.
In her arms, he found his rest,
A love that burned within his chest.

In the realm where embers softly sway,
A fire elemental found his way.
The womanizer, once untamed,
Reveled in the love he'd gained.
He traded fast flames for a steady glow,
A passion that continued to grow.

She Rises

In the quiet moments of dawn, she rises,
Rises to face a world painted in hues unseen.

She rises with patience, a gentle dawn,
Dawn of understanding, where differences are
embraced.

She rises to the symphony of challenges,
Challenges that echo in the corridors of her
heart.

In the labyrinth of neurodiversity, she rises,
Rises with unwavering love, a beacon in the
unknown.

She rises with courage, a quiet strength,
Strength to navigate the unique journey they
share.

In the tender hours, she rises,
Rises with hope, a sunrise of possibilities.

She rises to the rhythm of acceptance,
Acceptance that dances in the eyes of her child.

With every sunrise, she rises,
Rises as the steadfast guardian of a beautiful
soul.

In the trappings of motherhood, she rises,
Rises as the unwavering advocate, the fiercest
ally.

With each dawn, she rises,
Rises to the chorus of love, undying and true.

With the heart of a mother, whose child dances
to a unique melody,
She rises.

They Linger

In every whispered breeze, they linger,

In the rustle of leaves, they linger,

In the sunrise's golden hues, they linger,

In the silent night, they linger,

In the echoes of laughter, they linger,

In tears that fall like gentle rain, they linger,

In the quiet spaces of solitude, they linger,

In the twinkle of stars above, they linger,

In the depths of our hearts, they linger,

For though they left this earthly sphere,
Their essence remains, forever near.

In every moment, in every place,
They linger.

Ode to my Friend

Ode to thou, thou beacon bright,
A constellation in life's starry night.

In the tapestry of time, a cherished thread,
Thy presence, a blessing, where'er it's spread.

Thou art the sunlight in my darkest hour,
A constant source of strength and power.

Through life's labyrinth, hand in hand we tread,
With every step, by loyalty led.

Thou art the compass when the path is unclear,
Guiding with wisdom, my friend so dear.

Through seasons of change, a steadfast tree,
Thou art the roots, anchoring me.

With shared dreams and secrets untold,
Thou art the confidant, precious as gold.

With gratitude and love, this ode I send,
To thee, my dearest and truest friend.

Nexus

In a realm where mana's threads entwine,
Elementals arose, guardians divine.
Earth, a giant, both grounded and wise,
Made mountains by hand, reaching the skies.
Water, a fluid song in rivers and seas,
Tells tales of tides, carried by the breeze.
Fire, a tempest, in the heart of the blaze,
Wore flames that dance and amaze.

Air, a maestro, with ancient insight,
Guided the birds in their joyous flight.
Together they sensed an imminent plight,
An apocalypse looming, an upcoming fight.

Earth quivered with unease,
Water whispered warnings on the seas.
Fire roared, a fierce, untamed desire,
While Air hummed a melody, a symphonic lyre.

United they stood, a council in the night,
A cosmic alliance against impending blight.
Yet, the imbalance spread, a threat so vast,
A dark force rising, a shadow cast.

In the nexus ethereal, where powers combine,
The Elementals convened, a pact to design.
To stop the End, they must explore,
A new element, "Spirit," to heal and restore.

The elements wove, their powers entwined,
A dance of creation, pure and refined.
From the fusion of strength and unity,
Spirit emerged, a force of divinity.

Spirit, born in the cosmic expanse,
A unifying essence, their mana enhanced,
It bound the elements in a mystical blend,
A power that the apocalypse couldn't rend.

With Spirit, they faced the encroaching night,
Balancing the mana, restoring the light.
The dark force waned, as their powers
combined,
With the alchemy of Spirit, victory they'd find.

Elementals, keepers of nature's accord,
In their union, harmony was restored.
Now the elements, triumph in hand,
As guardians of balance, forever they stand.

Dear Brother

It has been 25 years already, since you first
opened your eyes and greeted the world with an
innocent smile. Your life hasn't been an easy
one. You learned quickly that your legs and arms
didn't work quite like everyone else's. All you
wanted was to be able to run and jump and play
like the other kids.

Thinking different.

Sounding different.

You didn't want to be different.

Your beautiful brain that absorbs any
and every speck of information about any and
everything that interests those you love. Your
monotone voice that you force emotion into. I
have seen your struggle. When you can't roll
your eyes so you roll your whole head instead.
When you nervously pick at your short strands
of facial hair. When you belt out a genuine
laugh, bubbling up from the gut. I see you.
When Christmas comes, and your face holds no

expression, but your hands are shaking with excitement. Others might not see, but I do.

Even though I have to look up at you now, I know you still look up to me. You might not know it, but I look up to you, too. Life has been tough for you, but you hang in there despite it, greeting me much like you greeted the world when you first emerged… with an innocent smile, and eyes that don't quite meet mine. I see your struggles and your triumphs. You feel alone sometimes, like you will never be understood. I may not ever fully get what you've gone through, but…

I'm here, like I always have been.

And I always will be.

www.ingramcontent.com/pod-product-compliance
Lightning Source LLC
La Vergne TN
LVHW021327200726
843509LV00014B/2426